Visions of My Soul

Inspirational Poetry

By
Martha Jenkins Newson

Copyright ©2011 Martha Jenkins Newson

This publication is designed to provide competent and reliable inspirational information regarding subject matters covered. No part of this publication may be reproduced, stored in a retrieval system, or transmitted, in any form or by any means, electronic, mechanical, photocopying, recording, or otherwise, without the prior written permission of the author, except for brief quotes used in review.

Library of Congress Cataloguing-in-Publication Data has been applied for

Publishing Consultant:

Deborah M. Smart
http://www.gladstonepublishing.com

Publication Date: January, 2012

ISBN-10: 1-928681-24-7
ISBN-13: 978-1-928681-24-3

Printed in United States

Dedicated to

My devoted husband, Calvin Newson who went to be with the Lord, November 24, 2002. I thank you for a wonderful life.

To my daughters, Laura Bryce, Carol Ellis Mitchell and Carmen Newson, my devoted special child.

To Yaphetti Stones (my nephew who God gave me) I love and I thank you for your faithfulness because you are with me every day.

To my grandchildren who I love:

> Laila Thompson, Wanda Ramnath, Elijah Pitts, Glenda Neal, Wadeeah Ellis, Irvin DuBois, Brittney Mitchell, Warren Lee Ellis, Lisa DuBois and Brian Rainier Mitchell.

And finally to all of my nephews, nieces, and other family members, I love you.

To God be the glory for the things He has done.

Introduction

My name is Martha Newson; my maiden name is Jenkins, which I am proud of. I am the daughter of William and Madeline Jenkins. I was born January 22, 1930. My mother said my sister Careatha, Helen and I were born in a house--1261 in Pattan Street, South Philadelphia. Then she and my dad moved to 2708 Latona Street in South Philadelphia, when I was 9 years old. There was eleven of us; Careatha, Helen, myself, William, Pauline, Andrew, Orangelee, the twins--Walter Lee and Leroy, Madeline and Robert. We were a happy family. Christmas at our house was a day to remember.

I loved school. I went to Benson Elementary School, which is torn down now. It was on the corner of 27th and Wharton, in South Philadelphia, and I attended Audenreid Junior High until I graduated and went to South Philadelphia High School for Girls and graduated in 1948. It was not co-ed then. There was a South Philadelphia High School for Girls and a South Philadelphia High School for Boys.

I graduated from Community College and received my CDA (Child Development Association) certification. I taught pre-school at 2515 Germantown Avenue at the Philadelphia Parent Child Center. I also have a credential in Early Childhood Education from Temple University. I received an award from the Senate of Pennsylvania for Good Citizenship. I have been a Block Captain for over 50 years.

I have been called the "Poet of Greater Exodus Baptist Church" where I have written poems and been an active member for 26 years.

I was blessed to have a loving childhood and a strict mother who raised us to love the Lord. She had a motto she raised us with, "Don't you never look down on anyone unless you are picking them up." I raised my children with that same motto and they have been blessed also. Poetry comes easy to me, because it is a gift from God. I'm thankful that I can still write at the age of 81, and I am still clothed in my right mind. Thank you Jesus.

1st Corinthians 1:9 *"But as it is written, Eye hath not seen, nor ear heard, neither have entered into the heart of man, the things which God hath prepared for them that love him."* KJV

I pray that my poems can reach inside someone's heart and make a difference.

Martha Jenkins Newson
August, 2011

Acknowledgement

I want to thank and acknowledge my Lord and Savior for allowing me to write this book, for without Him I can do nothing and I am nothing. With God, all things are possible.

I want to thank Zola Aminata who introduced me to Deborah Wilson Smart, my publishing consultant, who designed the cover of this book and arranged its entirety. This book would not be complete without acknowledging Reverend Dr. Herbert H. Lusk, II and his wife, Sister Vickey Lusk, my Pastor and First Lady of Greater Exodus Baptist Church. Pastor Lusk labors in the Word daily to feed not only my soul, but the souls of thousands wherever he goes. I want to thank Sister Vickey because of the years that I spent with her in my home and for her encouragement to keep writing for the Lord through poetry. I also thank Pastor's son, Herbert Lusk, III because at Pastor's 24th Church Anniversary Pastor asked me to be his guest at his table; and his son Herbert said these words to me, "Sister Newson, when are you going to write a book of poetry?" I said to him, "One day 'little pastor'." I always called him that since the day he was born. I never called him Herbert. When I became a member of Greater Exodus, Sister Lusk was pregnant with Herbert.

I also acknowledge the Greater Exodus Baptist Church family who was given to me by God and especially my Sunday School Teacher Sister Queenie Hinton Williams, who has been an inspiration to me as I have become a Sunday school teacher sitting under her for many, many years. When she teaches the Sunday school, the bible comes alive.

I also acknowledge those who helped me with this book; Deacon Michael Upshaw and Deacon Fred Smelley and all of my other deacons who have always helped me; to Bobbi Jo Coles and Nicky Moreland for their support; the West Poplar Neighborhood Advisory Committee (NAC). I want to thank Dennis Meloro at Nationwide Auto Repair Company Ruth Antonetti, Anna Marie Forte, Mary Carter and Amia Fisher who helped type my handwritten poems and Diane Smith and my daughter Carol Ellis Mitchell who helped put my poems in order and helped me make this book possible.

Robert Chisolm who bought me a black folder many years ago with over 50 plastic pages to keep my poems together, otherwise they would have been lost; I thank you.

I have been writing poetry for Greater Exodus for many years and now God has blessed me to write a book. "Thank you, Jesus."

Table of Contents

A Part of Me	17
Our Poems	18
Martin Luther King	20
Snowflakes	22
Say On	23
Twas Grace	25
Synonyms Forever	27
The Way Home	29
Trees of God	31
Black History Month	33
While We Have Time	35
Tough Times	37
God's Greatest Gift	38
Miracle of Flowers	39
A Book To Be Opened (Philadelphia)	41
A Marriage Blessed	44
Daughter	45
Mother	47
A Dear Friend	48
Family and Friends Day	49
The Warmth of Understanding	50
Black Woman	51
Father	53
How Do I Love Thee	55
Sitting at the Feet of Jesus	56
Remember Grandmom	57
Root of All Evil	58
Baby Talk	59
Reflections from Our Past	61

Baby Madden	62
The Cross	63
Philadelphia Ice Storm	65
Harlem Renaissance	66
Jenkins Family Picnic	68
Some People Never Look Up	70
Blessing From God	72
Waking Up	74
Wonders of Life	76
Art of Performance	79
Women of Greater Exodus	80
A Tribute to Pastor Reverend Dr. Herbert H. Lusk II	82
A House That is Orderly	85
Security	86
Growing Old	87
My Great-Grandson Danny	89
Portrait of a Christian Mother	91
Unwise Christians	93
This Cup	95
A Christian's Prayer	97
Show Love With Our Gifts	99
Psalm 139 – The Knowledge of God = My Letter to God	101
Martha's Poem	103
Motherhood	104
Barack Obama	106
Carrie	108
Calvin	109
Reason for the Season	111
He Has Risen	113

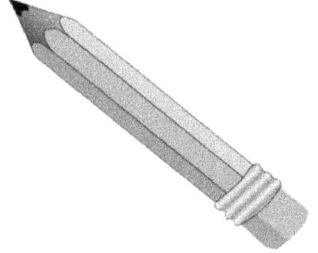

Poems to Remember

A Part of Me
Written January 22, 1996

Now that I'm seasoned in wisdom, my poems should be read.
To help someone along the way and lift a bowed down head.

In every poem I've tried to capture some warmth, some love and faith.
I've written each poem with joy seeing a smile on someone's face.

I've also had visions of everyone with love deep in my heart.
And I tried to write sweet poetry, for this is a gift from God.

So I say to you, who read my poems, open up your heart and see,
A part of me is a part of you and part of you is me.

Our Poems

Sometimes in life we often feel that no one really cares
A poem, a book, can reach inside, erasing shadows of despair.

Words are like medicine, they can heal and they can convict
The wise man reads and learns, the foolish remain foolish

As poets, writers and artists, let's keep this thought in mind
We can make a difference in the world, and establish a wiser mankind

When poems are written with compassion, man will read and have a plan.
Mankind becomes more friendly because now they comprehend.

Yes our poems can live in everyone, and
we can take them near and far.
We act upon the strength from them no
matter where we are.

Children love to read fairy tales, youth
love romantic things.
The elderly love to remember, hoping to
see another spring.

So poems should relate to everyone reviving their yesterdays.
Let's write each word so the world might
know our poems are here to stay.

Martin Luther King

Written January 15, 1985

Man born of woman
has a short time on earth.
And to give one's life,
who can measure its worth.

The depth of this man's love
was deeper than time.
For he lived and died
for a better mankind.

Many weary and troublesome days
he survived.
But the faith in his heart
kept his spirit alive.

So come on Philadelphia,
let the word Brotherhood flow.
In your homes, on your jobs,
get on board Boat House Row.

From the North to the South,
from the West to the East.
Feel the love Martin felt,
as he prayed for World peace.

Snowflakes

How gently each snowflake falls,
caressing with care.
Like a flock of miniature birds
floating in the air.

Continuously they fall, landing,
no one really knows.
Leaving their heavenly traces
descending from above.

Snowflakes you're a wonder
each a different shape.
Like the people here on earth
fading and unique.

Keep falling little snowflakes
covering our cities and our streets.
Making patterns for all of us touching
the strong and the weak.

How you flutter falling sideways
with a breeze of your own.
Letting nature beauty once more know,
you're heavenly owned.

Say On

Did you say on earth today
what God wants you to say?
Or were you persuaded
to listen to Satan's evil ways?

Did you smile at someone,
or did they see a frown?
When your help was needed,
did you adhere or did you let them down?

Do you practice what you preach
or just look and step aside?
Are you a Dr. Jekyll in the daytime,
and at night a Mr. Hyde?

Do you go to church on Sunday
with love in your heart?
Or just to whisper slander
and critical remarks?

When we examine and see ourselves
for what we really are.
We become fruitful branches
on the mighty vine of God.

So say on and preach the gospel,
win souls and you will see.
The light you show will surely glow
bringing love and victory.

Twas Grace

Twas Grace that leads me all day long,
twas Grace that sets me free
Twas Grace that lets me lead a life,
to win all victories

Though trials and mountains block my
view, I know there is a way
To tear them down and see beyond a
clearer, brighter day

A valley green, a snow cap mountain or
lilies in a field
A voice that speaks within my soul, dear
child just only yield

Take now my hand, I'm always there,
you'll never be alone
I carried you your whole life long,
from me child do not roam

Repent believe I'll never change,
today or yesterday
I wash you clean just ask me to,
as you kneel down to pray

For wisdom joy and understanding,
is still within your reach
Reach out and lean on me today,
I'm here to grant you peace.

Synonyms Forever

Glow candle glow casting shadows
on the wall
Glow candle glow dripping wax
as you fall

Aren't we alike both lighting up the dark?
We two have a purpose to warm
a broken heart

You're to glow and reveal your
ember beaming
Mine is to show love to those
who have no meaning

Though we burn slowly
we are still quite warm
Flickering brightly through
life's rough storms

Soon our flickering lights will cease
And then we both will find relief

Yours on the end of a candlestick,
never again to light
Mine resting in peace,
but burnt out with delight

The Way Home

I talked to my Heavenly Father today,
who sees and knows all things.
It's a privilege to feel the joy and the peace
His presence always brings.

Prayer changes things for everyone – if we
truly pray in faith, mountain move,
burdens cease and love replaces hate.

When we read the Bible, God talks to us
and shows us how to live,
we learn what we must do in life to be forgiven and how to forgive.

What wisdom the Bible shows to all, what
understanding God's Word reveals,
search every page and you will find that
Jesus through God did heal.

We too have power if we take up our
cross, and follow The Word of God.
Put our feet on a rock, cleanse ourselves,
and let our conscience be our guide.

Be filled with the Spirit and walk in it,
that's all that Jesus asks;
for He is The Way, The Truth, and The
Life – we all must walk this path.

In order to see God's smiling face when
we stand before Him one day.
Start now repent, reach out for Him,
He's waiting for you today.

Trees of God

Even the trees recognize God,
why can't man
They wave their leaves in thankfulness
whenever they can

They drink the dew, embrace the rain
growing ever tall and strong
Welcoming God's little creatures
extending them a home

Why can't we share what God
has given us here on earth?
Can we shelter one human being
who needs a sleeping place?

Lord let us be as your great trees
bringing shelter from the storm
Ever grateful for your miracles
of life in many forms

And then we will be rooted
like your great majestic tree
And all may see us as the branches
you meant for us to be

Black History Month

Each month of our lives think Black
History Month for we are a race who
survived. Through success of the defeat
of slavery and yet we are still alive

God gave us the Grace to be a great people
and to prove to the world our worth.
We're kings, queens and scholars first
humans here on earth.

We should never be ashamed of who we
really are, just search and you will find
we're great leaders, educators, scientist
born with regenerating minds.

So let's take each month for the rest of our
lives and make each moment count.
Make your mark in the world for all to see,
do your best to really surmount.

We already have all we need
God has given it all to you.
Just ask my people and the Lord will supply and he will surely see you through.

While We Have Time

There is a time to live and
there's a time to die
A time to say hello and
a time to say good-bye

Also a time to sit and
a time to take a stand
There's a time to reach out and
hold somebody's hand

We never stop to think
with each ticking of the clock
that our time on earth
will soon be ticking out

Let's search ourselves and make amends
for we all make mistakes
Forgive one another while we have time,
love heals, hate hurts.

Let's give thanks unto our Mighty God
that he woke us up today
to live upon this earth
to fellowship and pray.

So I leave these words with you
just seek and you will find
That in each of us deep in our hearts
is a love for all mankind.

Tough Times

Tough times never last
but tough people do
Determination when things are rough
and the Lord will see you through

Each trial and tribulation
is a test we must not fail
For each mountain that we climb
leads to a smoother trail.

Put on your whole armor of God
look up toward the hills
There is a light to lead you on
and a voice that says be still

Wait on me, be of good courage
and I will strengthen your heart
Take my hand, lean on me
from you I won't depart

Aren't you glad for tough times,
we seek and we have found
the love of God and happiness
as we stand on firmer ground.

God's Greatest Gift

How precious is baby Jesus,
born on Christmas day,
He came into this world that sinners may
be saved.

Just think about this precious gift,
God gave to you and me.
For through His blood we are redeemed
and we have the victory.

Over all that comes against us,
this tiny babe did come,
reaching out his hands to all,
God's only begotten son.

Be thankful for God's gift of love
Who'll never leave your side.
Rejoice and remember – He is Jesus
and He's God.

So when you open your gifts,
on this great Christmas day,
open up your heart to Jesus
for His love is here to stay.

Miracle of Flowers

A flower is more than a petal,
a bud or a long green stem
Sometimes it represents ones' love,
in a time of sentiment.

Often roses mend a broken heart,
or extinguishes a burning feud
A telegram arriving with flowers,
quicken the love in I and you

There are numerous ways to view them,
one is to beautify our homes
And then we take them from the grave
in remembrance of love ones gone

Flowers speak to us in color,
they brighten up our day
And wait for us in florist;
whispering take us home today.

At Christmas time there are Poinsettias
in brilliant red they stare
Their color reminds me of the blood
my Lord and Savior shed.

A vase of lovely flowers,
sent to someone in distress
Soon eases their pain and sorrow,
replacing love and tenderness

Everyone should receive flowers,
while they are here on earth
For to inhale their lovely fragrance,
is like a tender warm embrace.

In all of God's creation,
we see his majestic power.
And, in the beauty of springtime
we see his miracle of flowers

A Book To Be Opened (Philadelphia)

The city where I was born
is more than home to me
The street where I was grew up
is so vivid in my memory

The snow in the early forties,
the shed roof on my mother's house
A cat named Tommy
always catching a little mouse

The snow ice cream my mother made
from God's bright glistening snow
and the quart of milk left on the steps,
the cream on the top so cold.

The Inquirer paper cost two cents then
was thrown on the marble steps,
the funnies that I read; Smiling Jack
always gave me pep.

The store named Orr's around the corner
sold chocolate Grade A's
They was square and smaller,
not like Hershey bar today

Cowboy Hill where I took my sled
to ride down a snowy hill,
praying to God to beat the train,
we thought then it was a thrill.

Our neighbor who lived behind us
or those across the street
were Italian, Black or Polish,
they were neighbors who were neighborly

The bakery on the way to school,
the aroma of fresh cheesecake,
I looked forward to buying it,
loving each bite I ate.

Audenreid Jr. High School,
gym was my favorite sport,
climbing the ropes I was good at,
exercising on the horse.

Then I graduated
from South Philadelphia High School
and said goodbye to all my friends.

Life only repeats itself
in your children and your grands.
I'm so thankful to God that He let me live
to remember all these things,
for life is a book to be opened
to read and read again.

A Marriage Blessed

First you must have understanding,
then your love will surely grow
Just listen to one another,
patience is needed to make it flow

Respect the feelings of one another,
keeps your love light shining bright
You are now one body ascending into
love's eternal light

Give warmth to one another,
keep faith always in your heart
God will see and touch your marriage,
He will bless it from the start

Daughter

What is a daughter to a mother,
when she is growing old
Well she's the one who warms her heart,
for she's music to her soul

She cares enough to say what's right,
bringing joy to her life
Who looks beyond her faults,
always giving her insight

She's the one who never procrastinates,
giving love that's right on time
Be ever careful to say the words
that makes mom's life sublime

Love in this world is not for sale,
it's given with delight
It doesn't cost a penny,
it's not darkness, it is light

A daughter is one who articulates,
with goodness in her heart
Who can make her mother see within,
without breaking her apart

Who seeks to do the things in life,
with respect each time they meet
Who face trials, with God in mind,
and the devil at her feet

If you're this kind of daughter
then there's love in your heart
And one day you'll have a daughter
who will be your shining star

Mother

Thank God that He did make for each of
us a Mother
Though Mom maybe a natural one
or chosen by another

A Mother is the one who's there in the
sunshine and the rain
Who knows our hurts and comforts us
through every trial and pain

She wants for us the very best
and prays that we will see
That God will always be our guide
if we listen and take heed

For those of us whose moms have passed,
thank God for our memory
For Mothers live in our hearts and minds
where ever we may be

A Dear Friend
Dedicated to Zelda Williams

It's seldom in our lives
we meet a tender loving soul
Someone who cares and takes
the time to share our heavy load

We realize they follow Christ
and He leads them every day
There is a light within their eyes, so bright-
ly it's displayed

You hear it in the way they talk
and see it in their smile
Their love it reaches out to you
and lingers for a while

They never change from day to day,
what a marvelous friend they are
You'll remember them wherever you go,
what a difference they made in your heart

Family and Friends Day

We love each friend
who took the time to fellowship today.
We know that you'll be truly blessed
for Jesus is the Way.

Just fill your mind with the word of God,
peace and love will flow inside.
Have faith in God's grace and mercy
and He will be your guide.

He is a friend who will never leave you,
no matter what you've done.
Give your life to Jesus,
God's only begotten Son.

Then spread the gospel that you've heard,
that others too may know.
You've been in the presence of Almighty
God by the little light you show.

The Warmth of Understanding

The warmth of understanding
is in the way we speak
Choose kind words to answer others
who confess that they are weak.

Strength comes to those who listen
to words of encouragement.
They feel genuine affection
from those who bring content.

Each time we help someone,
we know we've passed the test.
And the warmth of understanding
returns to us twice blessed.

Black Women

Black women,
strong, defiant, willing to achieve
Black women,
assertive, searching fulfilling her needs
Knowing she is a minority
procrastination is forbidden
Perseverance is the power
by which she is driven
She views herself as a person,
apart from sex and race
Her uniqueness is shown
in what she believes
She is the epitome of grace
Through life she's carried the weight
of many human denials
But her proud black spirit soars
towards brighter tomorrows

Seeking wisdom and understanding,
she looks forward with no regrets
Separation did not negate her pride,
to exceed and gain respect
When forced to
she can show great strength
both mental and divine
But beneath it all she's soft and firm,
a legend in her time.

Black Women

Father

Father is the one who sets
the values and goals.
He acts upon the faith
that's deep within his soul.
He loves family unity,
his wife is his help meet,
and his children are his image;
revealing righteousness he'll teach.

He strives to meet all obligations
his family needs in life.
He works for his children,
and his love is for his wife.

The young man's glory is his strength;
the old man's beauty his gray head.
Behold his wisdom comes from God;
his salvation and his bread.
Yes, even if he's deceased,
his love will live on in the hearts of his
children and all of his loved ones.

Lord, we thank you for our fathers
our daddy and our friend
And we thank you for the memories
for he will always live in them.

How Do I Love Thee
To My Husband Calvin Newson

With every breath that I do take
With every step that I do make

With every smile upon your lips
With every touch from your fingertips

With every blink from my brown eyes
With every thunder in the skies

With every sunshine the earth might see
That's how much I do love thee

Sitting at the Feet of Jesus

Sitting at the feet of Jesus
and listening to His Word ---
We see a vision of Mary
and the Gospel that she heard.
Goodness and Mercy is at His feet
as we humble ourselves and pray.
His compassion faileth not
and new mercies come our way.
As women of faith, we please Him
when we live honorably.
Sitting at the feet of Jesus
is the place we long to be.

Remember Grandmom

I never knew my Grandmom
or saw her lovely face in a picture
or an album, never felt her warm embrace.

But I believe on Mother's Day
somehow she feels my love,
as she watches me from God's blue sky
from heaven up above.

Grandchildren call your Grandmom
remember her on Mother's Day.
Each day is a day to call her,
let her feel your love always.

Don't be guilty of neglecting her
for she has wisdom just for you.
There's a special love inside of her
for Grand's and children too.

Take time from your busy schedule
reach out and make a start,
fill a void inside Grandma's soul.
Show love to an aging heart.

Root of All Evil

The love of money is the root of all evil
it binds the souls of men.
Their greed to gain the worldly things
can only bring them pain.
They lose the love of those in life
who are near and dear to them,
while they only seek to cheat and steal,
making enemies not friends.

Some call themselves Christians
but they live not a Christian life.
They worship silver and gold
not our Savior Jesus Christ.
I pray for them who foolishly
just throw their lives away,
and hope they see the treasure
God has planned for them one day.

Baby Talk

If every baby could speak at birth
we all would be surprised
For they would say such funny things
to make us realize

For instance one would say,
"Thank God, I now can see the light."
Another one would say,
"Oh boy, I wasn't laying right"

Still another one might say,
"Stop Doc, I'm sure your heard me cry."
"Stop spanking me on my rump,
can't you see tears in my eyes."

A tiny one might say,
"Hey Doc, you better put me back.
She expected a boy and I'm a girl,
just find the water sack."

Another one might say at once,
"Stop holding me upside down.
Take off that mask you make me laugh,
you look just like a clown."

But we all know babies can't talk
but my how they can cry.
We love them all, they smell so good
they're the apple of our eye.

Reflections From Our Past

We honor you African-Americans
your names were hidden so long
You've excelled in war, peace and work,
you've made this country strong.

The sweat, blood and tears you've shed
makes us competent and great.
It's understood we're a strong black vine
no system can eradicate.

We're a sought out nation under God,
who brought us thru triumph and pain.
The memory of your achievements
gladdens the hearts of us who remain.

We are constantly gaining more
knowledge of who we really are.
We're an original nation, led by God,
we're his bright and morning stars.

Baby Madden

A baby is a precious thing,
expected on this earth.
It binds the love in families
as we look forward to its birth.

Babies live within its mother's womb.
Nine months of precious time.
We count each moment till their born
with love stayed on our mind.

Baby Madden,
what a joy it is to call your precious name.
My sister she is here today,
in spirit she will claim.
The love she would have shed on you,
it is already done.
Through God's own Spirit
you are welcome – precious little one.

The Cross
Written April 19, 2002

Must Jesus bear the cross alone
and all the world go free?
No, there's a cross for everyone
and there's a cross for me.
So as we bear our cross in life,
remember we're not alone.
We have a friend in Jesus,
God's only begotten Son.

He knows our trials and tribulations
nothing is hidden from his eyes,
just ask and He will answer
for He's a loving and merciful God.
"Praise Him" for He bore the cross
salvation it is free,
Yes, in His blood we are renewed
and we have the victory.

Whatever in life is troubling you;
just leave it at the cross.
Jesus rose with all power in His hand,
saving sinners that are lost.
The cross, the cross, the cross.

Philadelphia Ice Storm

Lord as I look
through my kitchen window,
I see two icy trees;
a rainbow of flickering lights,
oh what a sight to see.
Each limb just seems to welcome your sun,
wet branches reach to pray,
they seem to whisper as they gleam,
Lord, let us live today.
Though several branches are torn down
so many left are strong,
the rooted trees depend on you
to keep it all day long.
If only man could be rooted
and grounded Lord in you.
This mean old world would turn around
and all would be renewed.
Lord, touch your people so we can be
shining rainbows in our life.
No Christmas tree can glow like yours.
Icy trees reflect heavenly light.

Harlem Renaissance

A time when Colored Negroes
then progressed and thought anew.
Their gifts and talents recognized
independent businesses grew.

The Charleston Step, Cotton Club, light
skinned dancers were the thing.
Still struggling migrating from the South,
many came to Broadway and fame.

Not as buffoons but talented men,
audiences raved and realized.
Their skin was black and underneath were
souls that were alive.

With faith in God, Harlem became a new
land from oppression.
Now great desires to survive,
no longer feeling total rejection.

They knew they only had a slice of the
white man's apple pie.
But they kept on keeping on,
with bright tomorrows in their eyes.

Welcome Black History Month
we've earned our place on the map.
We're inventors, artist, kings and queens
we've excelled with honor and tact

Jenkins Family Picnic
Written August 24, 1996

Lord touch our family picnic
for we've come both near and far.

We ask for love and unity,
may it penetrate each heart.

Let this be a new beginning
for our family today.

For it is not what we do,
but so often, what we say.

Let's remember those who passed
with love now in our hearts.

A family should be forever
not a picnic in a park.

Martha Jenkins Newson

This may be the last picnic
for some of us here.

Whether you are young or old,
you're not guaranteed next year.

Get to know all your relatives
and search yourself and see.

That no matter where you live or go,
you are part of the Jenkins' tree.

Some People Never Look Up

Some People never look up
unless there's sunshine or rain.

Some People never look up
until there's sickness or pain.

Some People never look up
unless there's trouble in their house.

Some People never look up
till they lose a relative or a spouse.

And then some people never look up
even though they have a need.

Others never look up
it's just too hard for them to believe.

Some people never look up
they are just too busy in this life.

Some People never look up
till they miss the glory of God's light.

I write this poem to tell you
look up towards the hills;
and you will feel God's presence
and hear a voice that says "be still".

Blessing From God
Written August 24, 1996

If you need a friend who never fails,
well Jesus is His name.

He'll answer if you call on him,
for He will never change.

He's the answer to all our problems,
whether they be big or small.

He waits for us to talk to him
and He answers every call.

He can deliver us from anything
that is against His will.

He's the doctor in your sick room
and His word will be your pill.

He'll cover you with His blood,
all your burdens will melt away.

Peace and joy will be your path
for His light will lead the way.

So, come on God's people
just thank and praise His name.

Then let others know, wherever you go,
He can make them whole again.

All we have to do is trust him,
wait on him and read His word.

In scripture there is an answer
to every problem in this world.

So, let us all be thankful
for the goodness He has done.

For we can't find a friend
so faithful as our Lord, the Holy one.

Waking Up

I woke up tired this morning,
but God was on my mind.
I thanked him for waking me
to see the bright sunshine.

I knew he had his hand on me,
as I knelt down to pray.
I shut my eyes and asked the Lord
to guide me through the day.

I felt a warmth within me,
I knew that it was God.
I saw my Jesus on the cross
and suddenly I cried.

I know that I'm not worthy
for all the pain you bared.
But show me Lord just how to love
and how to really care.

Look down upon thy servant
and use me Lord today.
Walk with me, take my hand,
and teach me how to pray.

And suddenly I wasn't tired,
instead I sang a song.
He looked beyond my faults
and I became so strong.

I sang and sang unto my Lord
and praised his mighty name.
I'm looking forward to tonight
and waking up again.

Wonders of Life

Have you ever stopped to wonder
that nothing really dies?
When a rose withers in the winter,
in the spring one is revived.

If a friend disappoints you,
another will take their place.
If we travel across this nation,
we see a love one in a strangers face.

Have you ever stopped to wonder,
the good seem to suffer more.
While the rich gather more riches,
hardly ever considering the poor.

Have you ever stopped to wonder
what makes a strong man cry?
And how quick a baby falls to sleep,
hearing a soothing lullaby.

Have you ever stopped to wonder,
why a barking dog won't quit;
until he is yelled at by his master,
who called his name so quick?

If all these things amaze you,
then listen to this thought.
You're never considered a criminal,
until at last you're caught.

Have you ever stopped to wonder,
that no one wants to die.
But we all fall short doing the things
we should, that might prolong our lives.

Have you ever woke up
in the still of the night
and read the Bible
which filled you with delight?

Well that is just the wonder
of the mighty hand of God.
For He's the one who leads us
with his staff and his rod.

He's the answer to all our plights;
he sees and knows all things.
In him we find, if we just seek,
the love that knowledge brings.

For in life there are many wonders
that face us every day.

But the Living God of this universe
will direct us on our way.

Art of Performance

We can make things happen,
if we try and do our best.
Remember if we fail we try again
for it is just a test.

A trial we all will conquer,
if we persevere and strive.
This is what each one must do,
in order to survive.

Performance is a part of life,
we live it every day.
We can fight the good fight,
in all that we display.

Believing, giving and receiving
is performance for success.
To be accepted for who we are,
searching for love and happiness.

So the art of performing
is not what we supply.
But what we are and what we become
is the artist in you and I.

Women of Greater Exodus

Father, you've planted within us
your purpose for eternity.
We claim all your promises
as women of integrity.
Our mission is to serve you
in a powerful new way.
In everything we do Lord,
and in everything we say.
As we kept the faith dear Lord,
you have answered every prayer.
Lord you gave the increase
saved souls are everywhere.

In the choir, Women's Breakfast
and every ministry I see;
Sunday school, Children, Youth, Adults
and the faithful Elderly.
Father, we know we are your children
as we lift our hearts to you.

Lord, we feel your passion,
as your love comes shining through.
As Women of Greater Exodus,
we have sought and we have found love,
power and the beauty of holiness;
as we stand on firmer ground.

A Tribute to Pastor Reverend Dr. Herbert H. Lusk II Going from Good to Great

The ancient of days hears our Pastor as he preaches. The love of God is in his heart you can feel it as he speaks.

In Pastor's eyes there is a light that guides him day by day. He has visions for his people as he kneels each time to pray. I've seen the Power of God's Spirit and his love upon this place.

God's anointed ones are chosen at the time of their birth. Pastor Lusk labors in the word so our lives can be made whole. He speaks the truth about himself so each of us can search our souls. We've become more than conquerors as we've listened to God's Words. Obedience is better than sacrifice when we have evangelized what we've heard.

When our Sanctuary was burnt with fire Pastor seen beyond the smoke. God restored our sanctuary for he never gave up hope. When we needed to pay off our mortgage God blessed us, it was paid. You should have seen Pastor's face as he thanked God and prayed. Then Pastor spoke to the congregation and said we needed central air. Many Saints gave cheerfully for they know Jesus never fails.

Pastor then asked us to be faithful and give to the Reggie Fund. Therefore our Sanctuary can become larger and keep Satan on the run. Each of us in this Great Church is blessed with Pastor Lusk. Many have gone from welfare to work, for in God they put their trust. Each Christmas thousands receive turkey baskets and can food for all. But first they are fed the Word of God and saints are being called.

Now we're blessed with a Credit Union, People to People Charter, Computer School, Hope Center, The View and more saints; twenty-nine active ministries, faithful deacons and reverends. Praise God's holy name.

Pastor now has taken a stand for Africa, again he gave a helping hand. Seeing through the eyes of God he has a love for every land. It would take so many pages to record what our Pastor's done. Behold it's only what we do for Christ that will last until He comes.

Going from Good to Great, Happy 28th Pastoral Anniversary, Pastor Hebert H. Lusk II, we love you!

A House That is Orderly

A House should not be just a building
with steps, bricks and walls.
It should represent where our hearts live
and true love conquers all.

This should be a place where we feel
comfortable after working all day long.
A place to eat, sleep, communicate, warm
our feet and sing a song.

Where the sound of our mate and children
fill the hearts of young and old,
and where there are no mate and children,
loving animals warm our souls.
Our house represents our personality
and the way we feel inside.

If it's cluttered up, our minds are too
and we're struggling to survive.
But when we get our house in order,
our minds and hearts agree
that a House that is filled with peace and
love is a House that is orderly.

Security

Like a ship sailing to safe harbor
is a mind that's stayed on Christ.
Like a baby clinging on mom's breast
is certainly their delight.

Like many receiving their paychecks
anticipating to pay their bills.
Like a troubled soul who knows how
to pray and looks toward the hills

Like so many of God's children
who depend on his Word.
They rejoice for they believe every word
that they have heard.

So is a man who loves his family
and he works for them all day.
Every verse spells security
in each and every way.

Growing Old

Growing old is a privilege
Youth will never comprehend.

God gives us Spiritual Wisdom
as each day He takes our hand.
Through the years He's shaped and molded us as our lives are on display.

We know he is the potter
and we are just the clay.
Each day a chip or two will fall
because we're growing near
to be with our heavenly Father.

Those with faith they do not fear.
Our lives have been a journey
like a ship upon a sea.
Each month and year we traveled
sometimes in our memory;
we are grateful we've been favored
with Grace and happiness.

Our Lord has never left us
in every trial and test,
yes Growing Old is beautiful;
we have such memories.

In the daytime we relive them
in the night, sweet mystery.
Only those of us who have lived
Seventy Years or more
can realize what this poem means
and we are thankful to the Lord.

My Great-Grandson Danny

We thank you Lord for Danny.
He lived a little while (9 years old).
We are grateful that we knew him
and saw his loving smile.

He was a happy child Dear Jesus,
and he had so much to say.
I listened when I saw him,
Danny always made my day.

You chose him to be with you Lord.
God I know that you are wise.
We do not have the answers
and sometimes ask, why?

But I know you're in control
and your will shall be done
as sure as night brings darkness
and there is light in your bright sun.

Danny is in your presence,
Lord, as he is in my fondest dreams;
for faith is more than wishing
its evidence of things unseen.

Sometimes it takes a little child
to touch our very soul
and teach us Lord just how to love
and your beauty to behold.

I thank you for my Great-Grandchild
and what he means to me.
He's in your arms in Heaven,
where he'll be eternally.

Portrait of a Christian Mother

She prays because she loves the Lord
and knows He's always there.
Her heart is full of faith,
she knows God really cares.

She thanks Him for the blessings
he's bestowed on her life,
and whispers Lord help me
to be more pleasing in your sight.

Lord lead me to teach my children
to love and honor you,
comfort and keep them
all their whole life through.

Father touch my dear husband
guide his heart and soul to you.
Help him to see more clearly
and make his life anew.

Increase faith in my relatives
for some of them are lost;
cover them with your blood
you shed upon the cross.

Lord when we see each other
at the Judgment Seat of Christ.
Welcome me into your home
where eternity is bright.

Unwise Christians

How sad to enter the Sanctuary
not knowing whose we are.
We profess to know the Savior
but love from us is far.

Not thinking before we speak,
we deliberately seek to hurt with words
that are based with envy;
unruly evil then is heard.

In reality, they are insensitive
with malicious thoughts in mind.

They want others to think
they are doing good,
but they really are unkind;
judging others but not themselves.

They think they are in disguise
but nothing is hidden
from our Saviour;
He's Jesus and He's God.

I pray that unwise Christians
seek God's Kingdom in their hearts,
and as they ask for forgiveness
evil deeds then will depart.

This Cup

In my glass curio stands
sits a white antique china cup
covered with tiny gold leaves.

The leaves resemble tiny gold eyes
searching the room on every side.

This cup has been in the presence
of sorrow and grief, passion and pain
it has lasted through many seasons.

If this cup could talk
it would have an awesome story to tell.

This cup has survived fire,
water, earthquakes and storms.
This cup has never been broken.

Through time it has touched many lips
and held many liquids.

It has stood before wedding, birthdays,
graduations and anniversaries
and all holidays.

This cup is a conversation piece
its shape and beauty is unique.

This cup has belonged to one family name
for four generations.
This cup is a Family Treasure.
I love this cup.

A Christian's Prayer

Lord what shall I render
for all you've done for me.
Your agape love is so tender
and it's deeper than your blue sea.

There are not enough words
in an encyclopedia
or in Webster's dictionary,
to describe your awesome love
and all the souls you carry.

If I lived a thousand years
and saw a thousand stars each year
and stars could not outshine
how wonderful you are.

It's funny
when we've been through storms,
we seem to love you more.
You open doors and windows,
we have never seen before.

Your arms they hold us closer
as heavy winds do blow,
that's because you are a mighty God
and you did not let us go.

We are thankful Lord for safety,
what a wonderful God we serve.
You are Alpha and Omega,
the only living Word.

Show Love with Our Gifts

Love is a word
we speak from our lips,
but is shown in our lives
with these precious gifts.

The Gift of Remembering
those that we know,
with compassion and concern
when they're feeling low.

The Gift of Visiting
when our brother and sister are sick.

The Gift of a Phone Call
relieves pain so quick.

The Gift of a Card
you can send in the mail.

The Gift of Flowers
speak of love that is there.

When someone is missing
many weeks in the church,
it could be they're in need.
Ask, act and be alert.

Show love as our Savior
to someone in need.
It is better to give
than to always receive.

Psalm 139
The Knowledge of God = My Letter to God

Dear Lord,

Thou knowest all my thoughts and every path I've walked.

You know my down and up sitting, every word I've heard and thought.

Even when I lie down you know where I have been before I speak.

Dear Lord, you know each time I sinned.

I cannot comprehend thy knowledge it's too wonderful for me.
You're everywhere at that same time, from you I cannot flee.
Wherever I go dear Lord no matter what country or land;
If I take the wings of the morning even there your glory stands.

If I say the darkness covers me, your light shall be my light.
Nothing is hidden from you. You're the creator of day and night.
I am fearfully and wonderfully made. My soul you knoweth well.
When I was made in secret Lord, you delivered me from hell.

How precious are thy thoughts O' God, they are more than all grains of sand.
When I awake thou are with me, because you hold my hand.
I praise you Lord this day, as I call upon your name.
As you search me Lord knowing my thoughts, lead me to eternity planned.

Martha's Poem

Just say I did the best
I could in living in this life
I've done some good,
I've done some wrong
I wasn't always right.

I tried to show the love in me
to everyone I knew,
And strived to live a Christian life
in every way I could.

I want to be remembered
for the poems that I love,
As a mother who loved her children,
as only a mother does.

As a wife who loved her husband,
who was faithful to the end.
And a woman who loved Jesus
my dear unfailing friend.

Motherhood

Who can know the love of a mother,
only God can comprehend.
They seem by nature to be blessed with
wisdom and with strength.

When a child is first conceived,
they are then a living part;
for they rest beneath mom's breast
and listen to her heart.
When a child is born
she counts each finger
and counts each little toe,
and looks for a resemblance
as she kisses their tiny nose.

Already she plans their future
before it has begun,
and looks for God to guide her
for she has a race to run.

Even when her child is older,
and they have moved away.

They are always in her heart
and she prays for them each day.

They will always be her baby
no matter how old they are.
The love and care she feels from them
is higher than any star.

I thank God I am a mother
and know the joy that children bring.
It's a joy from God that grows and grows
each summer, each winter, and spring.

Barack Obama
Greatness on Your Shoulders
Written September 30, 2009

We who are not worldly
knoweth the deepest things of God.
We are spiritually discerned
and with Christ we're unified.
The Lord knoweth our thoughts,
and wise men are not deceived.
They are led by scripture
and follow what they believe
on the shoulders of great men.

President Obama,
there is a mighty weight;
but when we make a difference
that weight will make us great.
America is a portrait so beautiful to see.
Nothing matters more to all of us
than to live equally.
In this portrait, you can see every child,
woman and man. There is a struggle going on Mr. President.
I truly hope you comprehend.

As the people face their problems
we want to depend on you.
Each can tolerate their trials,
knowing their future will be renewed.

Most of us have seen the worse
because of the Republicans.
Sir, let them see the love in you
and how God has a plan.

More jobs available,
seniors secure in their benefits,
lower gas prices, taxes and increase in
programs paid for by our government.

Mr. President
please fulfill each obligation,
give the people what they need.

Behold, the greatness on your shoulders
will go down in history.

Carrie

Dear Lord we thank you for Carrie,
whose love stretched far and wide.
We thank you that she passed our way
with her pleasant, loving smile.

We ask that you just bless us
all who think of her and grieve.
For she had a way of opening doors
to those who were in need.

She touched the hearts of young and old
and found great strength in you.
We know she's resting in your arms
for she has been renewed.

Lord touch us all that we may live
to do your will on earth.
For it's only what we do for you,
will last and last and last.

Calvin

As I sit and think of all the years
that I have spent with you,
a warmth of love leaps in my heart,
memories they are renewed.

The way you use to wink at me,
in your own special way.
The memories of how you held me
tight at the end of each new day.

How many times did you tell me,
"you're gonna miss me when I'm gone"
I knew that you were joking then,
but now that time has come.

Not only do I miss you
and long to hold you tight,
in the daytime I'm so lonely,
I can't explain the night.

My arms they feel so empty,
I cannot hold you close,
but I can feel your nearness
and I live with that great hope.

Somehow I know our love lives on
in the quiet of the day.
In the stillness of the night
on my pillow you still lay.

I feel your arms around me
as tears fall from my eyes.
Death has only made me love you
more with every breath and sigh.

For in my heart you're in a pocket
and I have closed the door
to keep you there forever
until we meet once more.

*In remembrance of
my beloved husband, Calvin Newson.*

Reason for the Season
Written November 26, 1999

Each year when Christmas comes around
these thoughts they come again.
What shall I give my parents,
each relative and friend?

My children and my godchild
what gift will bring them joy?
I can't forget my best friends,
they had a baby boy.

I must remember my neighbors,
who live across the street.
I'll drop a card in their mailbox
and that will be their Christmas treat.

Can't forget my co-workers,
we work together each year.
Well, a basket of goodies
that'll be their Christmas cheer.

We meditate on all these things
and forget a tiny babe,
who came into this world
that sinners may be saved.
He reaches out his tiny hand
with love for everyone,
His eyes see everything we do
and He wants us all to come to Him
on Christmas day and each day of our life.

Behold, the reason for the
season is our savior Jesus Christ.

He Has Risen

He has risen
the resurrected and the life
He has risen
our saviour Jesus Christ

No man took His life;
He gave it up for you and me.
Resurrection was vital for our Salvation,
and we have the victory.

Jesus is eternal,
never to die again
or suffer for mankind
and take on their sins.

He has risen "Behold"
Jesus conquered death and removed
the sting of it
for that was God's request.
Our Lord has the ability
not only to raise the dead,
but become the resurrection
of the first fruit of the dead.

Christ came to bring a better hope
and it pleased God in all things
that Jesus would have *Preeminence*
with all power in His hands.

To understand the resurrection
we must believe the Father and the Son,
and when we study the Bible,
we know that they are one.
As many received our Lord
and serve Him in this life,
they will reign with Him forever
our Saviour Jesus Christ.

We welcome you Dear Jesus
on this Resurrection Day.
For you're the Only Living God,
The Truth, The Light, The Way.

He Has Risen!!!

Romans 8:28-31 KJV

²⁸And we know that all things work together for good to them that love God, to them who are the called according to his purpose.

²⁹For whom he did foreknow, he also did predestinate to be conformed to the image of his Son, that he might be the firstborn among many brethren.

³⁰Moreover whom he did predestinate, them he also called: and whom he called, them he also justified: and whom he justified, them he also glorified.

³¹What shall we then say to these things? If God be for us, who can be against us?

www.ingramcontent.com/pod-product-compliance
Lightning Source LLC
Chambersburg PA
CBHW070648050426
42451CB00008B/310